MY BOOK

Aaron Kavanagh

_____

To Keith
and
Charley

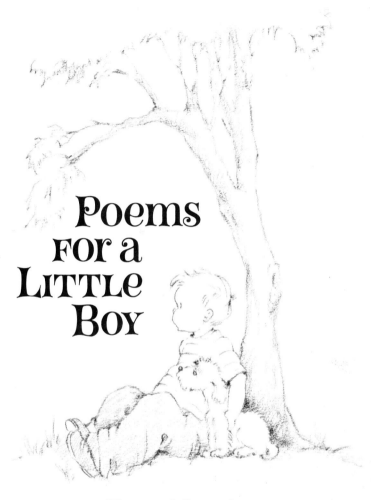

Poems for a Little Boy

Written and illustrated
by Anne A. Farrell

Stardust
Books

THE C. R. GIBSON COMPANY
Publishers
NORWALK, CONNECTICUT

MY STONES

I have a pocket full of stones
I found upon the sandy shore.
They make my trousers heavy
    on one side.
There're big ones, fat ones, shiny ones,
And little teeny tiny ones.
I found them where they'd washed up
    with the tide.

I take them out and count them all
When there's nothing else to do.
I like to feel their smoothness
    in my hand.
I guess the mermaids in the sea
Must have left them there for me,
My pretty, shiny pebbles
    from the sand.

Where Did the Wind Go?

I wonder where the wind went?
I think he wants to play.
He ruffled up my hair just now
And blew my hat away.

He whistled by so rapidly
I couldn't see him go;
He was in a dreadful hurry then,
For where I didn't know.

But he whispered as he hustled by,
"I'm going far away."
I can't remember where he said,
But he'll come back to play!

DRY LEAVES

Whisk, whisk, whisk on the sidewalk,
Whisk, whisk, whisk on the street,
Whisk, whisk, whisk
Is the noise they make
When I scuff through the leaves with my feet.

Leaves make no sound when they're falling;
They float down as quiet as snow.
I wonder what makes
Them crackle so
When "whisk" through the leaves I go?

Ants

Why is an ant?
Does anyone know?
He's always so busy,
So anxious to go.

He scurries about,
'Round and 'round,
Up and back,
In and out,
Up and over
The very same track.

He seems to get nowhere
Except where he's been,
And always ends up
Where he started again!

ICICLES

The snow was dripping off my roof
But never made a sound . . .
      Because . . .
It froze into an icicle
Before it hit the ground!

Cloud Pictures

Did you ever lie upon the grass
And look up at the sky,
And see a hundred elephants
Or horses riding by?

And while you watch the elephants,
They suddenly will be
A school of whales cavorting
On a big marshmallow sea.

And then a whale becomes a horse,
The horse a flying bird,
The bird an elephant again
With whiskers quite absurd.

The wind will chase the clouds around
And change them into fish,
Or dogs or pigs or submarines,
Or anything you wish.

And so I whisper to the wind,
"Keep blowing, so that I
Can lie upon the grass and watch
The elephants go by!"

RED BERRIES

Deep in the woods
    where the sun never reaches,
Close to the ground
    where the tiny things creep,
I found a berry,
    a tiny red berry,
Wrapped in a green,
    leafy cradle — asleep.

I looked at it long,
    and I wanted to pick it,
Lying so pretty
    and shiny and red.
But I left it — it seemed
    such a shame to disturb it,
Sleeping so cozily
    there in its bed.

THE ZOO

When Daddy takes me to the zoo,
Of all the things there are to do
I like the monkey house the best;
It's much more fun than all the rest.
The people laugh, the monkeys smile;
But still it seems that all the while

There's always one who'll sit and stare
At all the people watching there.

Of all the monkeys in the room,
I wonder who is watching whom!

WOOLLY SLIPPERS

I have my woolly slippers on.
I like to wear them so, becuz
My toes are cozy like a mole,
All warm and covered up with fuzz.

They're fat and fluffy like a muff,
They're squishy soft, with furry tops
And when I stand and look at me,
I look like handles on two mops!

Being Bad

I wonder why it's always bad
To scream and bounce upon the bed,
Or try to shave just like my Dad,
Or squeeze the cat when he's been fed.

It's bad to tease the girl next door,
It's wrong to scribble on the walls,
Or skate upon the hardwood floor,
Or in the living room throw balls.

I think it's really very sad
That things that seem such fun are bad!

FIREFLIES

I caught a firefly one night.
I put him in a jar to keep.
I thought I'd keep him for a pet
And told him to go right to sleep.

But every time I looked at him
He flashed a sad but hopeful light,
As if to say, "Do let me out,"
And "Please don't keep me here all night."

It seemed a shame to let him go,
But when I did take off the lid,
He flew straight out into the dark.
I lost him . . . and I'm glad I did!

Night Music

When I have gone to bed at night,
I like to lie awake
And listen to the drowsy music
The twilight creatures make.

The baby birds are ready
To be tucked into their beds;
Their mothers twitter gently
As they cover up their heads.

Far, far away I hear
The barking of a dog;
Down among the lily pads
The croaking of a frog.

The crickets play their violins,
The breeze is almost still,
And somewhere out among the trees
There calls a whip-poor-will.

The peepers sing their drowsy song,
A glow-worm holds the light;
And sleepy birds chirp quietly
A soft and sweet "Good Night".